Green Mountain

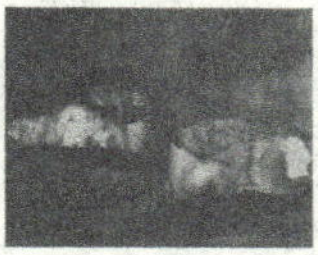

Poems by Yang Jian

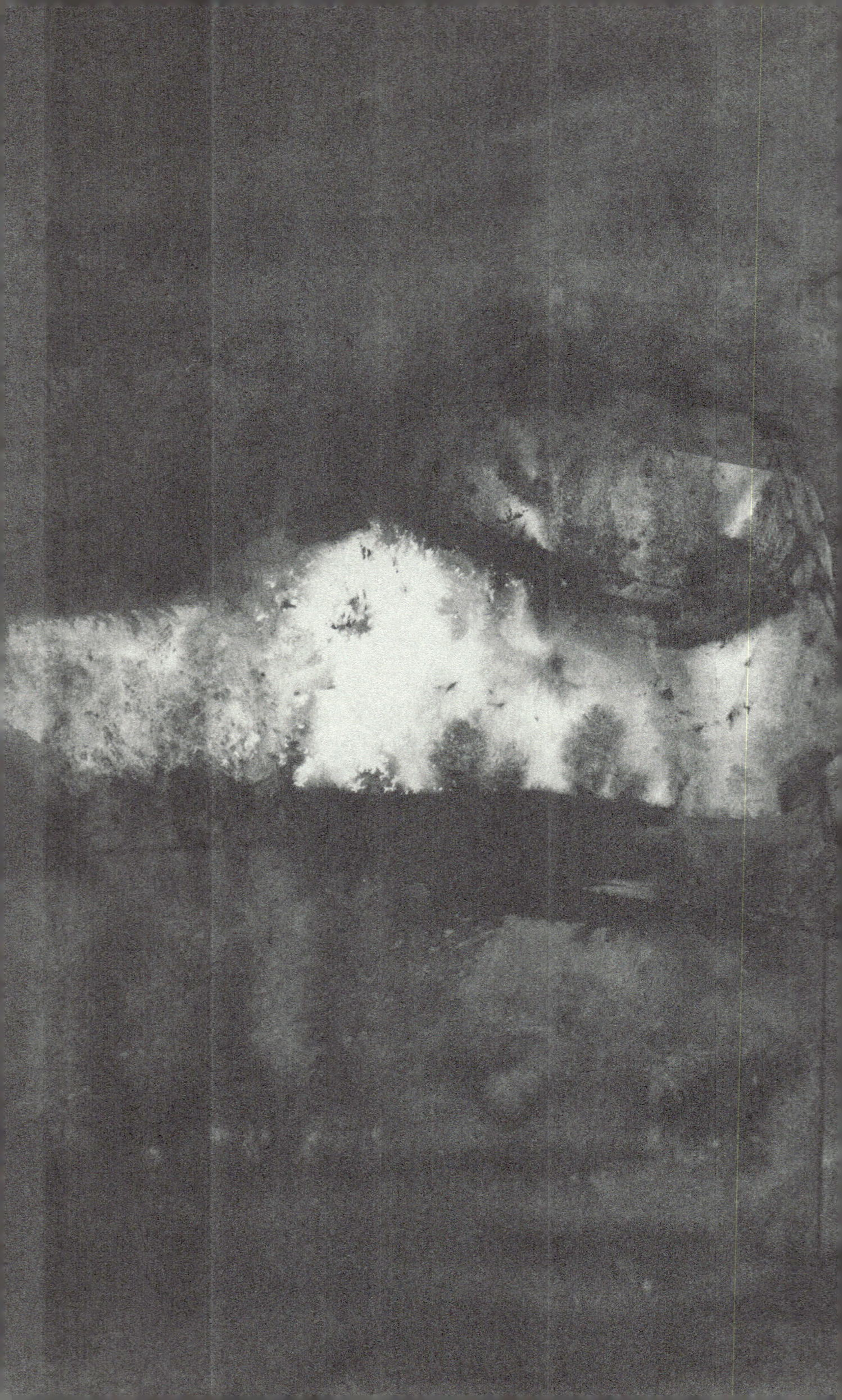

Green Mountain

Poems by Yang Jian

Translated from the Chinese by

Fiona Sze-Lorrain

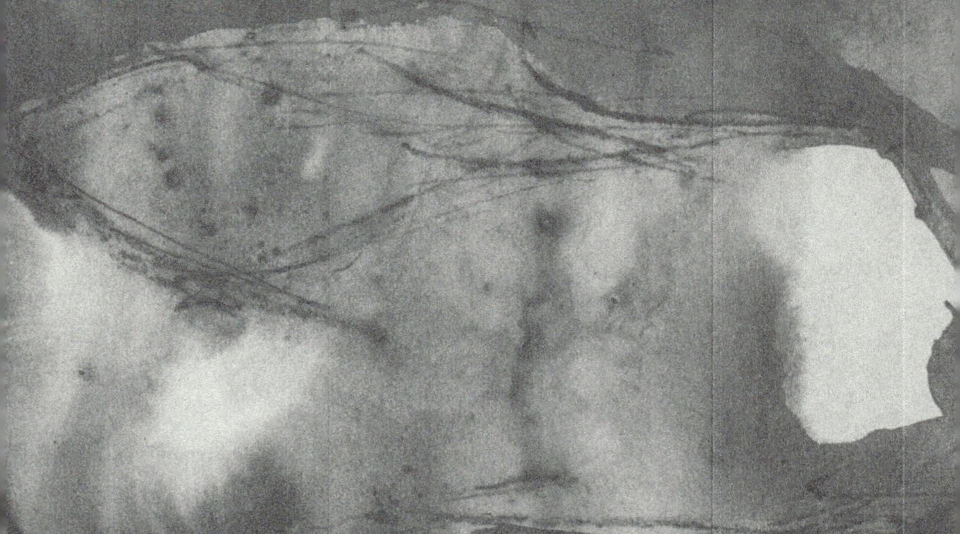

MERWIN ASIA

MerwinAsia
Portland, Maine

MERWIN
ASIA

MerwinAsia
59 West St., Unit 3W,
Portland, ME 04102
USA

www.merwinasia.com

Library of Congress Control Number: 2011944451
ISBN 978-1-937385-36-1 (pbk)
ISBN 978-1-937385-73-6 (cloth)

Printed in the United States of America

Cover and interior design by Lucian Burg,
LU Design Studios, Portland, ME
www.ludesignstudios.com

The paper used in this publication meets the minimum requirements of
the American National Standard for Information Services—
Permanence of Paper for Printed Library Materials,
ANSI/NISO Z39/48-1992

Distributed by the University of Hawai'i Press

Acknowledgments

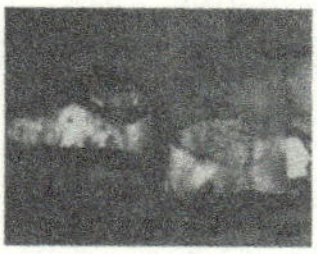

Grateful acknowledgment to the editors of these magazines in which several of the translations—in modified or earlier versions—have first appeared: *Antigonish Review*, *Bitter Oleander*, *Brooklyn Rail (InTranslation)*, *Cerise Press*, *Grain Magazine*, *Modern Poetry in Translation*, *Rattle*, *Vallum*, and *Words without Borders*.

The translator wishes to thank Bai Hua, Christina Cook, Sally Molini, Mark Strand, and Douglas Merwin for their helpful feedback and insights.

CONTENTS

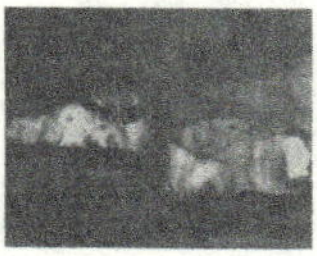

III SPEAK, HEART

Foreword

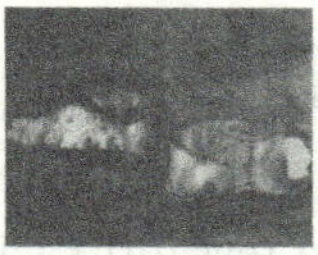

Christopher Merrill

“I was born in the foundering 1967,” Yang Jian writes of the Cultural Revolution, “destined to see everything with destructive eyes”—burned manuscripts, razed temples, the banishment of monks and nuns. And yet this remarkable poet, who understands his fate is “to open [his] mouth and speak among ruins / to open the iron door sealed by dust,” has turned Mao Zedong’s murderous legacy into a poetics predicated on his ability to see into the life of things. Through his Buddhist practice, study of Confucianism, and poetic gifts he has created a body of work informed by ancient Chinese spiritual values, which reminds readers that beneath what passes for a nation’s cultural and political life deeper currents flow, bearing not only literary riches but instructions about the meaning of our walk in the sun. “All my thoughts on immortality vanish in a straw hut / where the floor is made of mud,” he declares, and yet it is precisely here that the foul odor of tofu topped with rotten cabbage ushers him into the eternal present, where everything—sight and sound, breath and touch—counts. Priest of the visible and invisible alike, Yang Jian never misses a beat.

His translator, Fiona Sze-Lorrain, notes in her perceptive introduction that unlike other poets who “add in order to create,” Yang Jian works by means of subtraction, distilling the essence of whatever he chooses to write about—rain, a locked river tower, a fir grove at dusk. This is not unlike the method on display in the late landscapes of the American artist Georgia O'Keeffe, who would paint several versions of the same rural New Mexican scene, abstracting different elements until what remained was an essay in color and line. Yang Jian, who is also an accomplished painter, demonstrates this in the concluding stanzas of "Winter," a stirring meditation on the ways in which the frozen world can reveal the withering morality of an individual or a nation:

> Write down the bleak river
> Write down those fiery white reeds
> each dot a mountain peak
>
> each dot a shadow
> The river is painting with its murky expanse
> an empty victory after renunciation

Bridges, rivers, and mountains abound in this book, which correspond to crossings, currents, and sightings; at every turn there is a sense of possibility glimpsed, grasped, or thwarted; page by page, this book becomes a series of doors opening onto rooms that at a glance may seem familiar but upon closer inspection are quite strange. It is as if the poet draws from the deepest reserves of his language, culture, and tradition to portray the world in its infinite variety and all its uncanny guises. "In the dusk," he writes in a poem about a lost bat, "a hill path shines like a chain"—which is what links one thing to another, sentient and non-sentient beings alike. Here is a poet who can make a unified whole of the past, present, and future. Imagine that.

Introduction

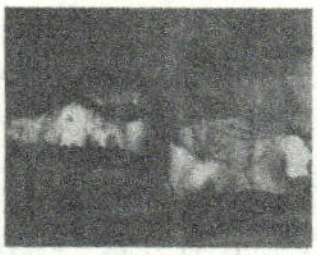

Some Novelties of Impermanence

Tracing the Floating World in Yang Jian's Poetry

Fiona Sze-Lorrain

At the risk of reducing a complex identity into an epithet, Yang Jian[1] often introduces himself as a Buddhist and poet. Despite his nationwide fame, translations of his work are scant, if not prosaic, in the current Anglo-Saxon world. But this does not stop certain Sinologists and unauthorized translators from mythifying Yang as a monk or a vagrant or a spiritual authority. It is true, however, that Yang Jian leads a semi-hermetic life in Ma'anshan, Anhui Province, upholds Confucian ideals, and adheres strictly to a Buddhist practice. After being laid off as a factory laborer, he has since earned a meager living through writing and painting. Aware of stereotypical connotations—and the exotic appeal—of a Buddhist identity, Yang finds ways to subvert biographical details for poetic abandon, both in spirit and language:

> I no longer seek
> I let go
> like dusk with its coolness
> the moon with its glow

---

1. Yang 杨 is the poet's family name, and Jian 键 his first name.

. . .

No longer seeking outward
when pain contracts
I let go

—"I No Longer Seek Outward"

"I no longer seek / I let go"—these are the words that struck me right away when I started translating Yang Jian in 2010. Neither an outcry nor a lament, each verse builds on an amplitude—a breath, a focus—at the end of it, and I can't help relating to the force and mystery of this inner world. This lucidity, so plainspoken, each line freely opening the space for embedded narratives to claim lyricism. Most poets add in order to create, but Yang Jian goes for the opposite: subtract. Pared down to its essence, the life of music now over, the love for life is felt in the bleak elegance of what seems like a hymn to impermanence. On the surface the honesty carries the beat of the verse, yet deep down it preserves the voice of a conscience that wrestles with expression. *This voice is real,* I told myself, *the writing authentic, its style natural.* How else to achieve this economy of words in a swift and light gesture, if not by speaking the truth, and from the heart?

Yang Jian's Buddhist faith is a defining aspect of his work. Whether the real in art triumphs over the art of the real, or that the latter outplays the former, Yang's Buddhist devotion never ceases to sustain his faith in truth, nourishing a poetic candor. Practicing Buddhism since age twenty, Yang was ordained in 1993 at the legendary Qixia Monastery in Nanjing. Since then, he has combined a meditative life with rigorous study in Confucianism and the classics. Still, his writerly journey comes with its own share of doubt and crisis. After his father's death in 1997, Yang Jian decided to stop writing poetry. Instead, he devoted himself fully to his spiritual vocation. When he renewed his poetic confidence in late 1999, he was by then deeply inspired and nourished by Jiangnan,[2] its tradition and charm. Yan Li, a Chinese avant-garde poet and painter who now splits his time between America and China, has this to say about his younger compatriot: "The true achievement of Yang Jian is the unity between his poems and his simple way of life. Working in the shadow of an overpowering feudal Chinese culture, he has resisted the temptation to live in a divided, schizophrenic way."[3] Probed by a journalist about distancing himself from the buzzing poetry scene, Yang Jian, surprised, offers an enlightening response:

> I don't like the word "isolated." How can man be isolated? There is always something happening that relates itself to him. Man and the world are one entity. In this sense, neither isolation nor solitude is possible . . . Distance, however, is an essential condition. It's required for cultivating *qi*, a quiet *qi*.[4]

---

2. Jiangnan—literally translated as "River South"—refers traditionally to the region and culture south of the lower Yangzi River. It comprises areas in Anhui, Jiangsu, Jiangxi, and Zhejiang, with cities such as Shanghai, Suzhou, Hangzhou, and Wuxi. Jiangnan is also an important cultural identity, a symbolic social construct, and popular historical imagination. Known for its high culture and refinement, it boasts of some of China's most exquisite gardens and landscapes.
3. Yan Li, "Thoughts after Reading the Poems of Yang Jian." *New American Writing* 24 (2006): 146.
4. Yang Jian, "Interview: My Innate Consciousness of Hardship." *Jingbao*. Shenzhen Press Group, 2008.

   I also refer to Simon Leys, who has written lucidly about the *qi* evoked by Yang Jian: "The literal meaning of *qi* is 'breath' or 'energy' (etymologically, the written character designates the steam produced by rice being cooked). In a broader and deeper sense, it describes the vital impulse, the inner dynamism of cosmic creation. For an artist, the most important task is to collect this energy within the macrocosmos that surrounds him, and to inject it into the microcosmos of his own work. To the extent that he succeeds in animating his painting with this universal breath, his very endeavour echoes the endeavours of the cosmic Creator." See Leys, Simon. "Poetry and Painting: Aspects of Chinese Classical Aesthetics." *The Hall of Uselessness: Collected Essays*. New York: New York Review Books (NYRB), 2013. 343.

Referencing Buddhism, Confucianism, and in few places Christianity in his poetry, Yang Jian writes to understand the human condition, not in terms of disparate situations or unique religious quests, but as a continuity since ancient times. In this regard, his theological sensibility is contemporary and global. In spite of its Buddhist ideals, his poetic world rejects the dominance of bodhisattvas, gods, and deities in the similar way that a Nietzschean *übermensch* does not function beyond its allegory and affirmation. Although in writing he cites bodhisattvas and evokes sacred places, the poet is cautious not to engage in an esoteric vocabulary that plays up to convention or ideology. Words turned fugitive become dust. In this way, Yang brings to mind the "Free Old Man" depicted by Japanese Zen Buddhist monk Musō Soseki (1275-1351):

His original way
  is plain and simple
    not caught up in things

He preaches the dharma
  at liquor stores
    and fish shops

He pays no attention
  to sacred rituals
    or secular conventions[5]

* * *

This bilingual volume, *Green Mountain*, contains a total of sixty poems, all chosen and compiled by Yang Jian and myself. Poems in the middle section, "Mysterious Gratitude," derive their doctrine mostly from the Confucian principles of

---

5. Soseki, Musō. "Free Old Man." Trans. W.S. Merwin and Sōiku Shigematsu. *Sun at Midnight: Poems by Musō Soseki* in *East Window: The Asian Translations*. Port Townsend: Copper Canyon Press, 1998. 220.

benevolence *rén*, propriety *lǐ*, righteousness *yì*, and harmony in an ideal hierarchical society. Portraits and personal lyrics drawn from autobiographical sources carry slightly more narrative drive in the first and last sections, "Ode to a Dead Tree" and "Speak, Heart." Overall, political agents are less acute in Yang Jian's poetry, "1967" being one of the most candid pieces: also an allusion to the poet's year of birth, it is a direct reference to the Cultural Revolution (1966-1976) and the ruins of China's spiritual plight. Others such as "Rape Flowers Seen from Jiangpu County to Shanghai" offer a slanted commentary on social illusions of the poor and the proletariat, whereas lines such as "We live in a great age of exposure" from the poem "Mount Zhen Monastery" suggest less oblique views of the contemporary civilization.

Yang Jian understands malevolence and a warring mankind as more a historical theme than a time-specific predicament of cause and effect. Such a belief, in part based on Confucianism, is fairly utopian, but more complicated and less categorical than what it might suggest: locked in conflict, Yang feels obliged as a disciple of the tradition to relay a corrective vision of humanity's state in the universe, yet the artist in him disparages his own poetry and its prospect of making a difference now and then; "Art isn't like a dead kin / letting man see the pretense of flesh," he confesses in "Locked River Tower," "I'm a man who looks at the river / My books, my poems can never lessen their misery." One may also surmise from poems such as "Years," "Speak, Heart," and "Remorse" that despite his Confucian discipline, Yang Jian has a difficult relationship with his kin and lover. Clearly it is not as straightforward as one assumes for the poet to shun oxymora, nor does a retreat guarantee a gratifying exit.

To honor the "purity" of language/music and restore the "essence" of speech/thought in my translation, I have made efforts to remove what Joan Didion once described as "veils of subordinate clauses and qualifiers and tentative subjunctives."[6] I would like to think that I am seeking to remove "aggressiveness"[6] or any form of "hostile"[6] presence that might give rise to abstraction or judgment, and possibly downplay the immediacy between the work and the reader. In an essay published in *The Washington Post*, American novelist Lily Tuck describes her writing credo that strikes a chord with me, "Adverbs are hills I must climb to get to my destination; adjectives are furniture blocking my way. English is a naming language; its power derives from nouns."[7] This awareness has helped me to access the tenderness at the heart of Yang Jian's linguistic inclinations without evoking sentimentality. It is not about exactitude, or minimalism, less so pinning down the *mot juste*. It is about something more sentient than elusive: a touch that reminds us of space and whiteness—but not emptiness, which translates into a fixed Buddhist concept.[8] Emptiness, if evoked in Yang's work, hopes to be understood as non-culture-specific, transformative, and far from being any form of absolute morality. As if to discount himself and his own didacticism, the poet has even laid bare his uphill struggle with emptiness in the poem "Surveying from Mount Dongliang:"

> None of these exists in the mountain
> Too much emptiness in the mountain
> I've yet to reach this emptiness

---

6. Didion, Joan. "Why I Write." *The Writer on Her Work*. Ed. Janet Sternburg. New York and London: W.W. Norton, 2000. 17.
7. Tuck, Lily. "Liars and Novelists Have This in Common: They Need to Sustain the Lie." *The Washington Post*. July 20, 2003.
8. At the beginning of the seminal Sanskrit text *The Heart Sutra*, the noble Avalokiteshvara Bodhisattva invokes, "Here, Shariputra, / form is emptiness, emptiness is form; / emptiness is not separate from form, / form is not separate from emptiness; / whatever is form is emptiness, / whatever is emptiness is form. / The same holds for sensation and perception, / memory and consciousness." See *The Heart Sutra: The Womb of Buddhas*. Trans. Red Pine. Berkeley: Counterpoint, 2004. 2.

Poems by Yang Jian are adroitly brief and simple—to the extent that words *feel* naked—in form, meaning, sound, and even appearance. Restraint and flow run parallel, dedramatizing each other in Yang's spare diction. But brevity enacts power and attention. It takes time to slow down enough to collect oneself and observe within the poet's reserves of feeling. As a result, drama grows within each frozen-frame scene: a static art with an antipodal story, which is the crux of Yang Jian's expression. I am thinking of the last stanza in the poem "Winter's Day:"

> Had we known we were two lambs
> on our way to the slaughter
> I'd weep, you'd also weep
> in this floating world

In this enigmatic piece, the poet does not view himself any differently from "a wild duck" that "cries on a lake one winter's day." Both of them are "alone and meek," vulnerable to a precarious end. The adjective "floating" in the concluding line creates a fluidity that heightens the subdued existential angst, yet the metaphor of life and destiny floating on water or in the air gives rise to a sense of lightness—perhaps a relief—and an elliptical erasure that inevitably leads to a period.

* * *

I have said nothing about the scenic beauty of Jiangnan or other places in South China, which in Yang Jian's work serve as portals to higher meanings and histories. A poet both intensely regional and universal, Yang does not shop for short-term refuge in these places of beauty and history in order to satisfy his existential needs. Instead, he forges for himself a space where nature tropes could humble the ego and tame the self. In *Green Mountain*, poems about dusk, mountains, and willows abound, whereby Yang Jian, the "Poet of Dusk" who eulogizes willows and bamboo, surrenders himself to the unfolding of questions of impermanence. "Truth comes from the observation of nature"[9]—so celebrates the Wabi-Sabi spirit. But Yang's poised odes, litanies, and elegies to Jiangnan carry another message more compelling in its implications: nature is not entirely at the disposal of humans. We pilot nature only at our own peril. Like prayers and psalms, these poems further define an eloquence that embodies music and echoes. My decision to minimalize punctuation and create blank spaces between words in these translations is part of a search for such eloquence and soundscape.

In my childhood, I visited Jiangnan. My memories are now a blur and fallible. But what has stayed with me—until today—is the feeling of being transported, in a state of weightlessness, into an ink and wash painting. For me, Jiangnan isn't a romantic cliché from fiction or films like Ang Lee's *Crouching Tiger, Hidden Dragon*; I have felt its otherworldly depth and presence on physical grounds. It came as no surprise to me, then, when I learned that Yang Jian is an ink and wash painter as well as a poet. On rice paper and in ink, he depicts landscapes of Jiangnan in the figurative and the abstract. Metaphorically and metaphysically, the visuals of Jiangnan in Yang's poetic world now challenge readers to house their imagination in both the concrete and the transcendent, the audible and the unspoken. In a manifesto, the 2000 Nobel Prize writer Gao Xingjian, who also leads parallel creative lives in literature and the visual arts, calls attention to the restorative power of painting, "A return to painting is freeing oneself of verbiage, restoring the concepts to language, painting where language fails. It is to begin painting where one has ceased

---

9. Koren, Leonard. "Wabi-Sabi Spiritual Values." *Wabi-Sabi for Artists, Designers, Poets & Philosophers*. Berkeley: Stone Bridge Press, 1994. 46.

to speak."[10] Along these lines, and to paraphrase the catchy memo from John Stuart Mill,[11] in an epoch when poetry needs advertisement to be overheard, I believe Yang Jian has returned to the heart of eloquence—by fusing lyric and landscape to reach the spirit. And through the fusing, reject the fusion, and trace the zero point.

---

10. Gao Xingjian. *Return to Painting*. Trans. Nadia Benabid. New York: Perennial (HarperCollins), 2002. 55.
11. In the first section of his essay "Thoughts on Poetry and Its Varieties" (1833), John Stuart Mill states, "[E]loquence is *heard*, poetry is *over*heard."

I

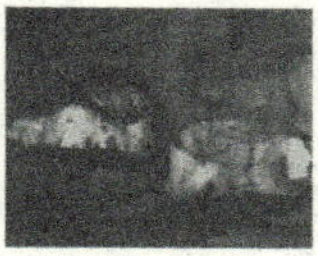

ODE TO A DEAD TREE

早春站台

乘客们一窝蜂挤向车门，
列车员大声喊着：“好好走！好好走！
摔倒了我不负责。”
他转过身，吐一口痰
小声嘀咕一句：
“ 再挤，不也是像拖猪一样。”
火车咣当咣当地走开了，
冒着粗重的白烟。

Station Platform, Early Spring

Passengers swarm to the train door
A train conductor yells, *Watch out! Watch out!*
I won't be responsible if you fall
He turns, spits
and mumbles
Come on, squeeze in, as if we were packing pigs
The train rattles away
in heavy white smoke

致山冈上一只孤寂的蝙蝠

狗叫声隐隐约约，
如点点泪滴。

山下
是胡乱盖起来的房子。

一只蝙蝠在飞，在山冈上飞，
快速、茫然。

薄暮中，
一条山路犹如枷锁一样锃亮！

To a Lonely Bat on the Hillock

Faint dog barks
like dripping tears

At the hill's foot
houses are built in disorder

A bat is flying above the hillock
speedy, but lost

In the dusk
a hill path shines like a chain

记录

在一条路上经过时，
一头正在吃糠的猪
把几粒糠甩到我脸上，
我想记录下这几粒糠，
却做不到。
我想真实地记录，
却做不到。

在山上，
有时，我也会像老牛一样
跪下来，
在我的脚上，
还有那拴我的绳子，
我想记录下这根绳子，
却做不到。

Record

Passing by—
a pig eating husks
throws some over my face
I want to record the husks
but I can't
I want to record them authentically
but I can't

In the mountain
like an old cow, I sometimes
kneel down
a rope
tied to my feet
I want to record this rope
but I can't

灰斑鸠

像一根带血的细绳子，
像一个抱着婴孩的穷母亲，
像窗玻璃上的泥点，
这是那片树林里灰斑鸠的啼声。

风大起来，
湖面昏暗、空旷，
我的生命
就要显露出来。

Collared Dove

Like a thin rope stained with blood
like a poor mother clinging onto her baby
like mud on a windowpane
this is the cry of a collared dove from the woods

Wind grows
The lake is dim and wide
My life
will emerge

何山桥所见

大桥下，
船工的打水桶，
被流水冲出很远。

一辆满载废铁的大卡车
驶上桥来。
两个快要被颠下去的农民工，
趴在那堆废铁上。
又一辆卡车驶来，
车厢里的铁钩子上，
挂满剖成两半的猪。
当卡车驶上大桥的顶端，
它们左右摇晃着。

一只鸟快速掠过，
“哇！哇！”
声音急促，
在天上
勾画着
何山桥下京杭大运河的灰暗奔流。

A View from Mount Ho Bridge

Under the bridge
a boatsman's bucket
is washed afar by the river

A truck full of scrap iron
crosses the bridge
Two workers on the verge of falling
sprawl over the scrap iron
Another truck passes
Pigs sliced into halves
hang on hooks
swinging left and right
as the truck reaches the other end

A bird dashes over
Wa! Wa!
Fast and urgent
it traces
in the sky
the dark rush of Jinghang Canal under Mount Ho Bridge

枯树赋

我没有一片叶子了，
只剩了刺，
这些刺不是我。
你们已经看不出
我是谁了，
我不会从枝繁叶茂沦落为一个简单的反抗者，
我活下来了，
而你早已变成我的反对者。
但你不要指望超过我，
你也不要指望超过我身边的这条大河，
更不要指望超过芦苇，
你甚至不能指望超过一片落叶，
落叶太美了，
没有声音，
你无法做到没有声音。
我最怕进步。
我保留了落后的、滋润的音调。
我枯萎了，
也在你心里盘根错节。
一旦我死去，
你们就滑落。

Ode to a Dead Tree

I've no leaf now
only thorns
These thorns aren't me
You no longer see
who I am
I won't be reduced from lushness to simple protest
I've lived on
and you're my opponent
But don't expect to outdo me
to outdo this river
or the reeds
Don't even expect to outdo a fallen leaf
It's too lovely
soundless
You can't reach soundless
I fear progress most
and keep a vintage, moist voice
I've withered
but still twist your heart
Once I die
you'll slide

雨

在狗毛、狗鼻子、狗眼睛里
在吆喝收垃圾的
拨浪鼓上

雨，洒下来了

在江水里
在校园里

雨，就像一个穷人
来到世上，
和屋顶上的另一个穷人
瓦楞重逢

在窗前，
雨是我的软弱，
雨，是伏在我肩上
哭泣的女人

多少年了，茫然哽在了咽喉，
我们连表达自己的感情都不会了。

Rain

In dog fur, dog nose, dog eyes
On the rattle
of a rag-and-bone man

Rain splashes down

into the river
on campus

Rain, like a poor man
arrives in the world
reuniting with another poor man
on the roof

By the window
rain is my weakness
It leans on my shoulder
a weeping woman

So many years, bewilderment clogs the throat
We even forget how to express our feelings

幸存者

人的言辞无法到达
一场秋雨下幸存
但已无法澄清的命运，
如同许多年前的恫吓依然存在。

他们睁着土灰色的动物眼睛
走在道路的一侧，
心里墓穴垒着墓穴，
面孔则是一片孱弱的荒草。

不论阴天和晴天，
他们都像在泥泞中。
他们以亡魂的姿态同亲人相处，
已经几十年了。

人的言辞无法到达
这样苍凉的雨声，
也无法到达
雨水中他们暗哑的面容。

Survivor

Language can't reach
a fate that survives autumn rain
Fate unclarified
survives like fear over the years

They stare with gray animal eyes
walk by the road
tomb after tomb in their hearts
their faces an expanse of weeds

Be it cloudy or bright
they seem drenched in mud
living like ghosts with their kin
for decades

Language can't reach
such bleak sounds of rain
can't reach
their washed-out faces

吴虔礼

下雨了，我挑着卖剩的豆腐从小镇往家里赶。

凭着鸟儿凄厉的叫声，
我看见它半空中雨水里晶亮的眼睛。
那一年

祖父挑着两筐线装书的灰烬去下葬，
他看着一船的字画渐行渐远，
并不觉得震惊。

我已摸到了笛孔，
但还不会吹，
现在最怕的是我还没有吹响笛子就已经死去。

风吹着我，
像吹着破芦席，
吹着运河上的烂菜梗。

那些死去的人太渴了，这些古树因而有了青苔。

Wu Qianli

It's raining—I carry the unsold tofu home from town

From its shrieks
I see the bird, its eyes glittering in the rain
That year

Without emotion Grandpa carried two baskets of book ashes
  to their grave
and watched a boat of words and paintings
drift away

I've found the flute hole
but can't play the flute
I fear death will arrive before I can play it

Wind blows me
like blowing a frayed reed mat
or rotten stalks by the canal

The dead are too thirsty: this is why moss grows on ancient trees

王若水

当我从河边的柳树学不会软弱的时候
我就死了
你并不知道

我是口死井
不通江河
在一个大的母亲的怀里

我忘了回去
学不会回去
也无人教我回去

夜夜出现的月亮
如一根仙草
我哽咽落泪也无用

Wang Ruoshui

Before a river willow could teach me how to be firm
I'm long dead
but you've no idea

I'm a dead well
no access to the river
in the arms of a big mother

I forget how to return
and can't learn how
No one can teach me

Moon that appears night after night
is an herbal grass
Even my tears are useless

敬一师

我扫落叶扫着扫着我就找不到家了，
一根细线一样的鸟叫声带我远去。
偶尔一根枯枝折断就是我了。
我又郁郁葱葱从不示人。

我早知，在河堤上佝偻
抱一捆柴回家给老母烧饭
是最美的事情。
我早知佝偻是人世间最美的动作。

竹子与我有何不同?
老梅枝与我又有何差别?
我波光粼粼，而群山如菩萨一样平躺，
我又枯败不堪从不示人。

Tribute to Master Yi

I sweep leaves and sweep away my way home
Like a fine thread a bird call lures me away
I'm a branch that breaks at random
I'm thriving but never show off

I've realized, to hunch on the dike
and carry firewood home to cook for my old mother
is the most beautiful thing
I've realized hunching is the loveliest gesture

How do I differ from bamboo?
How do I differ from an old plum branch?
I sparkle like waves and mountains lie like Buddha
I'm an utter failure but never show off

赵开聪（原名老人的死亡）

他的脚趾甲，
又尖又黄，
像墙角边
枯萎的槐树花。

他的肚子，
肿得很大，
像食堂里
翻扣的大铁锅。

不少人哭了，
为又尖又黄的脚趾甲，
为肿得很大的肚子，
不少人哭了。

几只苍蝇，
幽灵一样，
歇在老人的眼皮上，
赶跑了又飞回来。

Zhao Kaicong [originally titled "An Old Man's Death"]

His toenails
look sharp and yellow
like parched locust flowers
by a wall

His belly
swells
like a canteen wok
placed face down

Many of them weep
for his sharp yellow toenails
and swollen belly
Many weep

Ghostly
flies
rest on the old man's eyelids
flying back again when fanned away

1967年

他们说：
“ 这把二胡的弦要扯断，
琴身要砸碎。”
我们就没有了琴声。

他们说：
“ 这棵大树要锯断，
主要是古树，全部要锯掉。”
我们就没有了阴凉。

他们说：
“ 这个石匠要除掉，
那个木匠也要除掉，要立即执行。”
我们就没有了好看的石桥，
我们就没有了好看的房子。

他们说：
“ 这些圣贤的书要烧掉，
这些文庙要毁掉，
这些出家人要赶回家。”
我们就没有了道德，
我们就没有了良知。

我生于崩溃的1967年，
我注定了要以毁灭的眼光来看待一切，
我生下来不久就生病了，
我注定了要以生病的眼光来看待一切。

看着你们都在死去，
我注定了不能死去，
我注定了要在废墟上开口说话，
我注定了要推开尘封的铁门。

1967

They say
Snap the erhu's cords
crush its body
We'll no longer have its music

They say
Saw this big tree
Most of all, the ancient trees, saw them all
We'll no longer have shelter

They say
Get rid of this stonemason,
that carpenter too, right away
We'll no longer have exquisite stone bridges
no longer have exquisite houses

They say
Burn these manuscripts
destroy these temples
banish these monks and nuns
We'll no longer have morals
no longer have conscience

I was born in the foundering 1967
destined to see everything with destructive eyes
I fell ill soon after birth
destined to see everything with ill eyes

Seeing all of you dying
I'm destined not to die
but to open my mouth and speak among ruins
to open the iron door sealed by dust

岁月

1
几个得咽喉病的农民，
在芦苇荡边等着反绑之人倒地之后一哄而上，
他们的眼睛就像老牛眼，
老牛眼是一切眼睛中最可怜的。

2
你生路不走为何要走黄泉路？
我怎样劝也无用。
你好象在一个大的梦魇里我无法将你唤醒。
你白天睡觉，晚上活动，
父老乡亲对你这个穷光蛋的幻想，
一直过了很多年才破灭。
你身上有几百座上锁的大祠堂你根本不管
你生路不走为何要走黄泉路？

3
父亲年复一年进省城，
每回进省城，
他都要先坐半小时轮渡过江，
再坐四小时汽车。
这次回来他好象听懂了树林里灰斑鸠的叫声，
就像他的状纸
一再重复。
夜里有雨点，
扑向书页
有老哇子鸟在天上
一声、两声地叫着，
这是不是父亲呢？
他死去后在母亲梦里出现过十次，
在哥哥梦里出现过五次，
在朋友梦里出现过一次，
在我梦里出现过四次。

Years

1

Peasants who suffer from a throat disease
jump on the man with hands tied once he collapses by the reeds
Their eyes, like an old cow's
An old cow's eyes, the most pitiful eyes

2

Why do you choose death over life?
I coax you to no avail
You seem to linger in a nightmare, I can't wake you up
You sleep in the day, active at night
So many years, our parents
have given up on you
Hundreds of sealed shrines on your body, yet you ignore them
Why do you choose death over life?

3

Year after year Father visited the provincial capital
Each time
he must take a half-hour ferry
and a four-hour bus ride
Back this time, he seemed to realize dove cries repeated themselves again
and again, like his petition
Drops of night rain
rush into the pages
In the sky a crow
caws once, twice
Is that Father?
After his death Mother dreamed of him ten times
Brother dreamed of him five times
My friend dreamed of him once
I dreamed of him four times

父亲在进省城的路上啃烧饼，吃最便宜的阳春面，
随后在进省城的路上死去。
雨，
苦口婆心，
反复说着，
一件事情：
没有多少人再能透过自家的窗口
看见清闲的农田
从古圣先贤的教诲里
建立民族的信心，
没有多少人再去看一看
水面上恬静的荷花。

4

冬日的泥土
同来临的傍晚就像两个怀揣血汗钱的穷苦人，
在村庄里相遇，
晚风吹着湖水
也吹着家门口老牛身上
新生的绒毛，
好像天长地久并不是难事，
好像本来就是如此。
在很远的田埂上，
传来两个人清清楚楚的说话声。

On his way to the capital, Father ate pancakes and the cheapest
noodles
He died on the way
Rain
earnestly
repeats
this
Not many of us will see idle fields
through our windows
build national pride
with teachings of old sages
Not many of us will still look
at calm lotus on water

4

Dirt from winter days
And the coming dusk, like two poor men with their hard-earned
money
meet in a village
Night wind blows over a lake
and the old cow's
new fur
as if eternity was nothing tough
as if it had always been so
Two distinct voices
from a distant ridge

进省城

过长江时，
车上的乘客全睡着了。
汽车疾驶着，码头沉重的铁锈色留在了脑海里，
窗外的风景一掠而过。

惨白的石灰池边
有一台粉碎机。
在炸开的大山里
农民搬动着石块。

群山的灰烬
水泥厂的粉尘
在空气里
羞辱着田埂上的野花。

泥泞的乡间小路上，
衰老的农妇走过。
耕牛，
像一颗巨大的眼泪，立在草垛边。

烟囱插在麦地里，
在农家的红砖墙上，
用石灰写着:“少生快富奔小康”
“ 大打一场围歼车匪路霸的人民战争”。

而在省城，我会看见
另外一条江水
另外的，但是同样睡着的人们
像粉碎一样确凿！

Into the Provincial Capital

Over the Yangzi
passengers are all sound asleep
Car whizzing past, dense rusty shades of the harbor in my mind
Outside the window the scenery flies by

A pulverizer by a pale
mortar pond
Peasants move rocks
in a blasted mountain

In the air
mountain ash
dust from cement factories
humiliate wild flowers in the fields

Old peasant women
on a muddy village path
An ox
stands by the hay, like a large teardrop

Chimneys are planted in wheat fields
Lines written in lime
on a farmer's red brick wall, *Fewer children quick fortune and a good life*
Fight a people's war against road bandits

In the provincial capital, I see
a different river
men sleeping alike
as vivid as devastation

乡下记

在冬天，
乡下邋遢而枯黄，
一头牛的老实的身影，
不再是他们的遗产。

一个农人昨天死去了，
他臃肿的肚子，
和缩小的阴茎，
仿佛把人世的破绽泄露。

刚刚亮起的农家灯火，
更是渲染了
这里无穷的耐力，
和难言的寂静。

我们走着，奔跑着，
缓慢，缓慢的惩罚，
我们受了苦，
原是为了轻松地离去。

Country Chronicle

Winter
country, a shabby yellow
A cow's honest silhouette
no longer their heritage

A peasant died yesterday
His swollen belly
and shrunken penis
seem to reveal worldly secrets

Lamps brighten peasants' homes
enhancing
this boundless endurance
and difficult silence

We walk, run—
slow punishment, slow
We've suffered
for a light departure

喑哑

我活在一个大喑哑里，
那里的稻草生生世世在荒年里，
不管刮来什么风，飞来什么鸟，
喑哑依旧在那里，纹丝不动。

我身上有一座深宅大院被你忘掉了，
我身上有一座老码头被你掩埋了。
我记住了从天而降的雨水在锈迹斑斑的铁丝上落下，
我记住了南瓜花缠绕的一间铁皮屋子。

我活在一个大喑哑里，
我细小的身体里有一双临终的乌亮的眼睛，
也就是稻草窝里最不起眼的土青蛙的眼睛。
我死得早，但是没有关系

因为我的生命跟你们说的时间，
不是一回事。
我的声音的苍古之美被你们的抵抗之声践踏，
我有着难以延续的耻辱和悲痛。

Mute

I live in a big muteness
with straw in famine life after life
Be it wind or bird
the muteness stays untouched

You've forgotten a mansion in my body
buried an old harbor in my body
I remember rain off rusty iron wires
a corrugated iron house entwined in pumpkin flowers

I live in a big muteness
My small body contains two dying black eyes:
eyes of the ugliest frog in a nest
I'll die young, but it's fine

because my life differs
from your time
Your contending voices override the archaic beauty in mine
I've shame and grief that hardly lasts

古钟

浑身长满青苔的死猪，
沉睡着，好像一口古钟。

它要把腐烂呈现在这条河流上，
不允许我们把它掩埋。

偶尔，一只路过的细鸟站在它身上，
嘴里衔着一枚金黄的楝树果。

教堂里，头发花白的黄牧师
正在讲授耶稣上十字架时讲的那句话：

“他们干了什么，他们自己也不晓得。”
农妇们默默聆听，好像扶在船帮上落水人的手臂。

Ancient Bell

Dressed in moss, the dead pig
sleeps like an ancient bell

It displays its decay on this river
to forbid its own burial

At times, a small passing bird perches on it
with a golden neem fruit in its beak

At church, the white-haired Pastor Huang
preaches what Christ said when nailed to the cross

They know not what they do
Peasant women listen in quiet, like drowned hands clinging
    to a shipboard

香椿树

桃花已经开过了，
香椿的树叶在长出，
犹如孤儿头上
直立的几根毛发。

孩子们来了，
孩子们在放风筝。
山顶上的成年人，
看着进城的民工扛着苦水般的棉被。

从蚌埠来的穷人，
住在山坡上的茅棚里，
靠捡垃圾为生，
他们的妻子坐在嘎吱作响的竹凳上。

一朵无名的花，在山坡上盛开，
一缕残阳，犹如受难者
临近解放的泪滴，
洒在墙边的破瓦，车轮印上。

我还能干什么呀？香椿树……！

Toon Tree

Peach trees are past bloom
Leaves sprout from a toon tree
like the few strands of hair sticking out
from an orphan's head

Children are here
flying kites
From a mountaintop, adults watch workers
carry cotton quilts into the city, like carrying misery

The poor from Bengbu
live in mountain sheds
and survive by collecting garbage
Their wives sit on creaky bamboo stools

A nameless flower blooms on the slope
A last strand of light, like tears
of a victim soon free
scatters on broken wall tiles and car tracks

What else can I do? Toon tree . . !

II

MYSTERIOUS GRATITUDE

故土

当可以凋谢的时候，
我还是个孩子。
在古老而金黄的枫树林里，
我十五十三岁的样子。
像河水上温和的微光，
伴着镇河的小兽，
天心楼空阔的钟声。

Native Soil

When life could wither
I was just a child
In golden old maple woods
an image of me at fifteen or thirteen
Like soft river light
with a tiny beast soothing the water
and broad chimes from Sky Heart Tower

寒鸭图

山河、大地，
泉源、溪涧，
草木、丛林，
善人、恶人，

忽然变成水面上的一只寒鸭，
你就是用石头砸，
它也无家可归，
它本来无家。

Winter Duck Painting

Landscape, earth
springs, creeks
grass, woods
the kind, the evil

Suddenly—a winter duck in the water
Even if you hit it with a stone
it still stays homeless
It was born homeless

我曾想

我曾想，
要是我能说出自己的创痛，
我就安静了。

有一次，
一片被割倒的麦子说出了我的创痛。
它们被割倒时有一阵幸福溢出大地，
它们活着的目的就是被割倒，
它们被割倒时溢出的幸福说出了我的创痛。

一缕青烟也曾说出过我的创痛。
它是怎样说的，
我早已忘记。

如同一粒遗失在地里的麦子，
无法找到。

I Once Thought

I once thought
were I able to speak my pain
I'd calm down

Once
wheat spoke my pain
During its harvest, bliss spurted from the earth
Wheat lived for harvest
Its spurt of bliss spoke my pain

A strand of green smoke spoke my pain, too
How—
I've forgotten

Like a grain of wheat lost in the fields
never to be found

古老

我所有活不长远的念头在一间草屋里消散一空，
那儿的地面由泥巴所做。

柴火烧的大灶上，
煮着一锅白米饭。

两块豆腐在碗底，
烂掉的白菜盖在上面。

那臭烘烘又香喷喷的白菜似乎就是古老的中国，
我所有活不长远的念头在这又矛盾又统一的气味里消散
一空。

Ancient

All my thoughts on immortality vanish in a straw hut
where the floor is made of mud

On a huge wood-burning stove
a pot of rice is cooking

Two cakes of tofu in a bowl
topped with rotten white cabbage

The foul savory cabbage feels like old China
All my thoughts on immortality vanish in this contradictory yet
unifying smell

神秘的恩情

他们没有挖到水，他们在坑边虔诚地睡了。
睡梦中看见一条红鲤鱼翻进坑中，
水源源不断，井做成了。
我有幸生在一个真诚可以感物的国家，
我的泪于是滴在井沿上。
人啊，你一无所有，连井水都是红鲤鱼所赠，
你们都忘了，这故事也无人再讲述。

在这里，我祈求的安宁不过是护佑一位农夫牵着他的
老牛回家的暮色，
我祈求的智慧如同他手中悠然晃荡的牛绳，
我的泪要滴在这根牛绳上，
因为在秋天的时候我总是被一种神秘的恩情环绕，
这恩情世代相传，从未中断，
我生活在一个懂得连井水都是上苍恩赐的国家。

Mysterious Gratitude

They dug but found no water, so they slept piously by the pit
and dreamed of a red koi tossing in it
Water now runs, the well is done
I'm blessed to be born in a country moved by sincerity
My tears fall on the edge of the well
O man, you've nothing, even well water is bestowed by a red koi
Have you forgotten, no one tells this story anymore

Here, I pray for peace: dusk to protect a farmer
who returns with his old ox
Wisdom I pray for sways like his rope
My tears will fall on this rope
by virtue of a mysterious gratitude that enfolds me in autumn
Gratitude, unbroken through generations
I live in a country that knows even well water is bestowed by heaven

馈赠

树叶没有经过任何抵抗就落下了，
风，

又把它吹起，
它也是没有任何抵抗地“沙沙”作响。

在它瘦小，干枯的身体上，
爱，似乎比它在树干上的时候还要强烈。

是的，我是不死的，
也一定是这些树叶所赠。

Gift

A leaf falls without defense
Wind

lifts it up
Without defense, it shuffles again

In its thin, dried body
love burns stronger than on a trunk

Yes, I'm immortal
a gift from these leaves

锁江楼

铁船的一头浸在江水中，
岸边，每户人家的屋子里，
有一个活泼的孩子，一个残废的母亲。
艺术，还不能像逝去的亲人，
让人们懂得肉体的虚伪，
死亡闪现的微光。

几个民工在江边挑矿石，
有一瞬间，我真想跳下去
同他们一起干活。
但我站在楼上，
我是一个看江水的人，
我读的书，写下的诗，不能减去人们丝毫的坎坷。

Locked River Tower

An iron boat dips its head into the river
In every house ashore
a lively child, a handicapped mother
Art isn't like a dead kin
letting man see the pretense of flesh
the blink of death

Peasant workers are loading ore by the river
For a moment, I want to jump down
and work with them
But I stand on the tower
I'm a man who looks at the river
My books, my poems can never lessen their misery

祖国

枯草上的绵羊默默无言地望着远方，
多美啊，摆在油菜花地里的蜂箱。

一头眼泪般的牛拴在石头上，
拖拉机来回运着稻草。

那叫不出名字的鸟，在蓝天，眼睛，运河组成的灵魂里
飞过，
晒在春天里的冬日身躯，渗出幸福的汗滴。

我不了解运送石棉瓦的船工的苦水，
但是落在甲板，运河上的光，永存！他们乌黑的眼圈，
永存！

枯萎的荷枝犹如古人残存的精神，
没有什么比看到倒塌的旧房子更加令人难受。

姑溪河畔山顶的塔尖与江边码头的塔尖
同时，带着泥土的棕黄，刺向蓝天！

在车厢里，人们凝望着落日，
一件挂在桃树上的农民的蓝布褂。

Motherland

Sheep on dry grass gaze afar in silence
How lovely, beehives in rape flower fields

A cow like a teardrop is tied to a rock
A tractor moves hay back and forth

An unknown bird flies across a soul shaped by blue sky, eyes,
and canal
Winter bodies tan in spring, sweat in bliss

I don't understand the hardship of boatsmen moving asbestos tiles
Light on the deck and the canal is eternal! Their dark eye circles,
eternal!

Wilted lotus stems, like the ancients' morale
Nothing more tragic than to see old houses fall

Apex of Guxi River Mountain Pagoda, apex of the wharf pagoda
pierce the blue sky with ocher

In the train, people stare at the setting sun
A blue peasant shirt hangs on a peach tree

这里

这里是郊外，
这里是破碎山河唯一的完整，
这里只有两件事物：
塔，落日，
我永远在透明中，
没有目标可以抵达，
没有一首歌儿应当唱完。

我几千里的心中，
没有一点波澜，
一点破碎，
几十只鸟振撼的空间啊，我哭了，
我的心里是世界永久的寂静，
透彻，一眼见底，
化为蜿蜒的群山，静水流深的长河。

Here

Here are the suburbs
the only triumph of a broken landscape
Just two things:
pagoda and sunset
I stay forever in transparency
no destination
no song to end

In my heart of a thousand miles
there is no ripple
or rupture
O where dozens of birds flutter, I weep
My heart is the world's lasting silence
transparent, until the end
into meandering mountains, deep running rivers

乡村记事

为了我的成长，这墓碑上写着“爱妻刘氏”，
一个个长满杂草的坟墓，显然死去了全家。
为了我的成长，白墙黑瓦的小巷里
老叫花子的眼睛，像燃尽的煤灰。

一只病弱的山羊，像画中的耶稣，
站在臭水沟里，为了我的成长，
山坡上的残雪，仿佛未消的爱意，
那最远的江水，被更浓的雾气遮蔽。

Village Narratives

For my growth, this tomb reads *Endearing Wife Madam Liu*
Weedy graves sprawl, the whole family must be dead
For my growth, in an alley of white walls and black tiles
the old beggar's eyes look like burnt coal

A sick goat, like a painted Christ
stands in a foul drain, for my growth
old pastoral snow, like unfading love
the farthest river in a heavier fog

跃进桥

十二月的柳树，仿佛一个纤弱的小女孩，
我们要把她珍藏在心底。
远处的起重机勾勒着黄昏的凄凉，
一个工人和一个农民无言地相遇在桥头。

纵横的铁轨像放倒的绞刑架，
被落日的光涂抹着。
太像一笔债务，
要由我们来偿清。

郊外，一名贵妇人的坟上压着石头，
她的苦难从1912年开始到1990年结束。
她门上锁绊的“巴嗒”声
吞噬了一颗荒漠的心。

Great Leap Bridge

December willow, like a frail girl
We cherish her in our hearts
A crane from far traces a bleak dusk
A worker meets a peasant in silence on a bridge

Smeared with sunset
railways intersect like fallen gallows
like a debt
we must pay

In the suburbs, a lady's tomb lies under rocks
Her misery begins in 1912 and ends in 1990
A lock clicks on her door
and devours a barren heart

甑山禅寺

芭蕉的样子多么舒展，
狗跳着，咬身上的虱子。
当它叫累了，它会睡去。

小女孩翻看着睡莲叶子，
她的弟弟送一桶水去菜地，
在四周，群山像一件展开的僧人的袈裟。

几个农民刨开蒜苗地，
阳光涌入，
死者正是这样得到幸福的。

池塘里掏出来的淤泥，
摆在路边，
我们处在一个充分暴露的伟大时期。

Mount Zhen Monastery

How restful the banana tree looks
A dog leaps, biting at its fleas
Tired of barking, it will sleep

A girl flips over lotus leaves
Her brother carries a bucket of water to the fields
Mountains stretch like an open *kasaya*

Peasants dig a garlic field
Light pours in
This is how the dead are blessed

Mud from the pond
lies by the road
We live in a great age of exposure

在码头边

落日饱蘸着江水，沉下去……
江风吹刮着这些民工灰白的衣服，
他们还有一段江堤必须挖完，
其中还有两个蹲坐在石头上吸烟。

像是一桩大事已经过去了，
一种寂寞，同冬日的夜空很配，
人们在城里钉着铁窗子生活，
生命大部分被浪费了。

小牛犊跑起来，
一个痛苦的歪曲的器官，
在江水边低语：
“难道我是罪有应得……？！”

By the Harbor

Soaking in the river, the sun sinks
River wind blows workers' gray clothes
One part of the dike yet to be dug
two workers squat on a stone and smoke

Like a major event now over
a solitude fits the winter night sky
Men live in cities nailed with iron windows
their time mostly spent

A calf runs along
A suffering deformed organ
mumbles by the river
Do I really deserve this?

古桥头

万物在人的烦恼中
显得晦涩，不安而易逝。
麻雀像一阵污水，
飞回了柳树林。
这是我们的失败。
可怜啊，我们这些拒绝说教的猴子！
我们把哭声引入了
大好河山的祖国。
多么像我们自己，
金黄塔尖周围的蝙蝠。
钟声散成灰烬，
松树拧成铁丝，
落日像一个吻，
印在肺痨病患者的运河上。
田地没有耕种，
荆棘没有拔除……
什么也没有生下，
我们留给子孙的将是十分荒谬，
十分神经质的空白。

Ancient Bridge

The world in our distress
seems obscure, volatile, and fleeting
Like filthy water, sparrows
return to their willows
This is our failure
How pitiful, we monkeys who refuse teachings
We lure tears
into a glorious nation
So much like us
bats that surround a golden pagoda
Chimes disperse into ashes
pines twist into wire
Sunset is like a kiss
engraved on the canal of tuberculosis victims
Fields unplowed
thorns not pulled out
Nothing is born
We leave our children a very absurd
and neurotic void

古镇

听诊器挂在石灰墙上……
树荫下的老人扇着苍蝇，
小河像一枚生锈的针，穿过桥洞。
渔翁坐在船头吸烟，
孙女望着尖顶的水泥教堂，
采石矶门前的石狮。
一个税务员甩动着袖子，
从小巷的一头走到另一头，仿佛在说：
“你们这些奴隶
我的靠山很厉害的。”
菜筐里屈辱的西红柿
同仿古的仁义堂，遥遥呼应。
我们小时候的祠堂，
只有那棵大枫树还在，
它就像一阵寒冷，
加快了我们的脚步，
去看一位瞎了眼的老大妈。
她爱着枇杷叶的苦味，
房间的昏暗，
不幸是她唯一的洞察力。
在1950年之后，
人们丧失了欢乐的能力，
只有一些粗糙的
转瞬即逝的东西。

Ancient Town

A stethoscope hangs on the lime wall
An old man fans away flies under a tree
Like a rusty pin, the river passes through an arch
A fisherman sits on the bow, smoking
His granddaughter looks at the pointed cement church
the stone lion outside the quarry
A tax-collector swings his sleeve and walks
from one end of the street to the other, as if saying
You slaves
I've very powerful allies
Disgraced tomatoes in a basket
echo from afar the Hall of Benevolence
In our childhood ancestral hall
only a large maple tree survives
Like a gust of chill air
it hastens our steps
to visit a blind old lady
who loves the bitterness of loquat leaves
and darkness in her room
Mishap is her only insight
Since 1950
people have lost their strength to be happy
All that's left are some rough
fleeting things

古忠烈祠

仿佛我们的生命，
是春雨，
是淡薄的柳丝，
和脚下的青条石做成的。

而我们的思想，
就是月色下的瓦楞，
因为单调而无限，
下面有一个忠厚的屋檐。

低声谈论着这座建筑，
像谈论着一位死去了几十年的老人，
一棵古柏树的浩然之气，
一座老桥温婉的韵味。

Ancient Martyrs' Shrine

As if our lives
were made of spring rain
thin willows
and emerald stones under our feet

Our thoughts
are moonlit tiles
dull but boundless
over a sturdy roof

We discuss this architecture
like discussing an elder dead for years
the nobility of an ancient cypress
the flair of an old bridge

在东梁山远眺

在一棵老梧桐树下飘来一阵炖草药的香味，
我知道，这是我的祖国。
夜里将会有人把药罐摔碎在路中央，
我知道，我的祖国将会从药罐里流出。

跪着，
在这里跪着。
把胸膛里动荡的心，
跪成石像。

在炸出一个大口子的群山脚下，
有一截老柳树，就像龙的尸体。
在龙尸体周围是烧糊的青草。

山上没有这些，
山上的空白太多了，
我尚未到达空白的境界。

Surveying from Mount Dongliang

Pure herbal scent from an old phoenix tree
I know, this is my country
Midway at night, someone will smash a jar of herbs
I know, my country will spill from it

Kneeling
kneeling here
Kneel my restless heart
into a stone statue

At the blasted mountain's foot
an old willow stands, like a dragon corpse
surrounded by burnt grass

None of these exists in the mountain
Too much emptiness in the mountain
I've yet to reach this emptiness

开善桥

江水上的夕阳开始烧他了，
田野上沉沉的暮色就是他的骨灰。
母亲，这就是你的儿子
同你告别的方式。

你看，夜晚来了，
这正是他烧净的时候，
却留下这座桥，
怎么也烧不化……

Kaishan Bridge

He burns in a setting sun over a river
His ashes, a sunken dusk in the fields
Mother, this is how your son
bids you goodbye

See, night is here
right when he's all burnt
leaving this bridge
forever untouched

老祠堂

人们在老祠堂边煮着一个大牛头，
老祠堂里只剩下一棵银杏树了。

大牛头笑着，
在火上笑着。

因为它的血沿着家乡的小河，
流向长江，化作了江水。

你们相吻的嘴唇啊，
好像屋顶上的炊烟……

Old Memorial Hall

They are cooking a cow's head
near the old memorial hall where a ginkgo tree remains

The cow's head smiles
Over a fire it smiles

Its blood runs along our stream
to the Yangzi, and becomes river

O your kissing lips
like smoke above the roof

万年桥

陈大妈要死了，她让我明早去给她放一条红鲤鱼，
我捧着红鲤鱼去寻找万年桥下的那条河，
发现整座桥在大雾之中，我在其中迷失了方向，
我找不到河放掉这条红鲤鱼，
它在大雾中我的手掌上迷迷朦朦，不再动弹。
陈大妈很美，她的美，完全来自善良。
三天后她去世，我的嘴唇因此变成了神秘的草木灰，
　　从此无言。

The Bridge of Ten Thousand Years

Madam Chen was dying. She asked me to free a red koi for her
the next morning
Holding the koi, I searched for a river under the Bridge of Ten
Thousand Years
but got lost in the fog
I couldn't find the river to free this koi
In the fog it looked misty on my palm, and could no longer move
Ravishing Madam Chen—her beauty came from kindness
She died after three days. My lips have since become herbal ash,
mysterious and speechless

青山

山脚下池塘里的荷叶，
只有一点点干燥的声音了。
十几天的雪，
也没有遮住一片枯荷。

雪无边无际，
它比雪更无边。
它虽会变成一团烈火，
但这火不是它点燃的。

大片的云飞来，
一罐药
因灰暗而愈显湿润。

它在山顶打碎了，
寒冷而孤单。
一条小路静悄悄向上。

Green Mountain

A pond of lotus leaves at the mountain's foot
is left with a parched voice
Days of snow
can't even cover a dead lotus leaf

Snow is boundless
Vaster than snow
it can turn into a ball of fire
but can't ignite the fire

A fat cloud flies over
A jar of herbs
is dampened by darkness

It shatters at the summit
cold and alone
A quiet path climbs

III

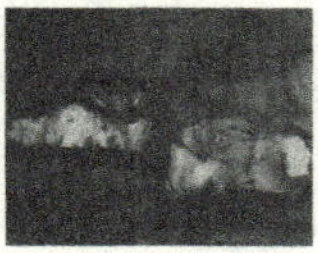

SPEAK, HEART

夕光

小时候，我在大堤上奔跑的时候见过江水上
渐渐西沉的落日，
长大后我才知葬身于它
又有何妨？
葬身，这大概就是我幸福的源头了。

当然，灵魂也可以细腻地存在，
比如墙头上枯草丛中的一只古瓮，
灵魂靠瓮盖上的一眼小孔，
靠暮晚时分的一缕夕光，
存活下来。

Dusky Light

When I was a boy, I raced on the dike over the river
watching the slow setting sun
Grown-up, I realize, *So what*
if it buries me?
Burial, the source of my joy

Of course, a soul exists in subtle ways
like an ancient jar in dead wall grass
The soul relies on a hole in the jar lid
relies on a strand of dusky light
to survive

哀诉

在田野里，
青蛙的叫声像是哀诉：
“我在一个坛子里，
在一个四条腿，两只眼睛的绿色小坛子里。”

Plea

In the field
frogs croak like a plea
I'm in a jar
a small green jar with four legs and two eyes

从江浦县去上海遇见大片的油菜花

过去，
我以为在大上海是见不到老人的。

过去，
我过长江，
以为一船的人都会表情严肃地看着这条
伟大的河流，
但他们都睡着了。
江水重复着，
他们逃避重复的唯一办法就是睡觉。
就像现在，
油菜花重复着，
他们逃避重复的唯一办法还是睡觉。
油菜花太美了，
从江浦县一直蔓延到大上海，
比外滩的帝国银行大厦，
美得多。

过去，
在我们穷人幼稚的想法里，
在大上海，
连人都是不死的。

Rape Flowers Seen from Jiangpu County to Shanghai

In the past
I thought old folks would not live in big Shanghai

In the past
across the Yangzi
I thought passengers would sternly observe
this great river
but they just fell asleep
Water repeated itself
Sleep, their only escape from repetition
Like rape flowers
repeating themselves now
Sleep, their only escape from repetition
So beautiful
they sprawl from Jiangpu County to big Shanghai
More beautiful
than the Imperial Bank on the Bund

In the past
we the poor naively thought
in big Shanghai
people were immortal

暮晚

马儿在草棚里踢着树桩，
鱼儿在篮子里蹦跳，
狗儿在院子里吠叫，
他们是多么爱惜自己，
但这正是痛苦的根源，
像月亮一样清晰，
像江水一样奔流不止……

Late Dusk

A horse kicks at a tree stump in the hay
Fish jump in a basket
Dogs bark in the yard
How they embrace themselves
the wellspring of sorrow
clear as the moon
running ceaseless as a river

山巅

落日以自己的无常向我们展示
化解痛苦的方法
蜿蜒的小路也来帮忙
还有草丛里星星点点的野花
在山下
烧荒的火焰
以浩瀚的流逝
也来提醒，来帮助……

Summit

In its disquiet the setting sun displays
its ways to resolve pain
A winding path offers help
with wild flowers sprinkled in the grass
At the mountain's foot
flames from slash and burn
offers help, a reminder
of their vast break

懂得

一座坟静卧着，
一块碑竖立着，
就像我自己在静卧，在竖立着。
风轻轻地吹过荒草，
一层一层地吹过去，
就像我自己在吹过去，
无动于衷地吹过去。
狗不断地在远处叫着，
又被寂静的虚空包容，
就像我自己在叫着，在包容着。
没有什么彼此，
也没有什么先后。
只有迷茫的人才会去伤害，
只有糊涂的人才会去憎恨。

Understand

A tomb lies quietly
A plaque stands upright
Like me lying flat, standing upright
A breeze blows past the weeds
layer over layer
like me blowing over
without emotion
A dog keeps barking from afar
embraced by a still void
like me barking, embracing
There is neither you nor me
neither soon nor next
Only lost souls wound
and muddled souls hate

冬天

在冬天，
人世凝成了
鹌鹑的瑟缩模样。

人世，喑哑了，
贯穿一个故事的浩瀚气息，
因道德的干枯而消失，

同衰败的风景，
难忍地相磨着，
像石头磨着胆。

他们没有养育孩子，
他们没有能力养育孩子，
他们想："不，还不能到此为止。"

记下江水的萧瑟，
记下强烈的白芦苇，
一点点山尖

一点点人影，
江水正用浩瀚的浑浊刻画
因放弃获得的空茫的胜利。

Winter

In winter
our world freezes
into a cringing quail

Mortal world, gone mute
A boundless breath weaves through a story
and vanishes as morals wither

It grinds in anguish
with ailing landscapes
like a stone grinding a gall bladder

They did not raise their children
They couldn't
They thought *No, not yet*

Write down the bleak river
Write down those fiery white reeds
each dot a mountain peak

each dot a shadow
The river is painting with its murky expanse
an empty victory after renunciation

我不再向外寻找

我不再寻找，
我放下，
像傍晚放下荫凉，
月亮放下清辉。

我们错了，
把希望寄托在外面的改变。
几年来，
被愤怒刺瞎。

阵阵思绪
像青铜器上的污垢。
抑制他们吧，
我们今生不幸和来世悲哀的祸水。

不再向外寻找，
在疼痛的收缩中，
我放下了。
月光撒遍了山顶。

I No Longer Seek Outward

I no longer seek
I let go
like dusk with its coolness
the moon with its glow

We're wrong
to put faith in external changes
all these years
blinded by anger

Waves of thoughts
like stains on bronze vessels
Let's suppress them
mishaps in this life and griefs from the next

No longer seeking outward
when pain contracts
I let go
Moonlight blankets the mountaintop

薄暮时分的杉树林

那里是一片片安谧的杉树叶，
那是历代游子的心。
那里逝去的一天天都静止了，
那里的安宁来自天上。

一条小径在树阴下伸展，
通向薄暮中的流水。
古代沉睡的智慧从那里苏醒，
死去的亲人，从那里回来。

Fir Woods at Dusk

There lie patches of calm fir leaves
hearts of wanderers over the ages
There fade days in stillness
tranquility from heaven

A path stretches under the trees
to waters of dusk
where ancient wisdom awakes
and dead kin return

薄薄的死叶在忘记

树林里的一阵清风在把她忘记
薄薄的死叶也在把她忘记……

在草木的代谢中，
有着劝慰我们遁世的古老律令。

我是暴雨过后清新的空气，
不属于一两个女人。

凋谢呵，你是众多艺术中，
最深奥，最难懂的艺术。

Thin Dead Leaves Have Forgotten

A breeze in the woods has forgotten her
Thin dead leaves have forgotten her

In the metabolism of nature
an old law urges us to live like hermits

I'm the fresh air after a storm
I don't belong to a woman or two

Ah fading, you're among all the arts
the most profound and cryptic one

山脚下

在埋葬圣人的山脚下，
民工们戴着只露出两只眼睛的灰蓝色帽子，
站在冒着白烟的石灰池边，
四周是狼狈不堪的田野。

好些年了，我不愿记录
在埋葬圣人的山脚下，
民工们戴着只露出两只眼睛的灰蓝色帽子，
站在冒着白烟的石灰池边。

At the Mountain's Foot

At the mountain's foot where sages lay
peasant workers wear blue-gray hats that reveal just their eyes
standing by a mortar pond of white smoke
surrounded by ruined fields

So many years, I don't wish to record—
at the mountain's foot where sages lay
peasant workers wear blue-gray hats that reveal just their eyes
standing by a mortar pond of white smoke

冬日

一只小野鸭在冬日的湖面上，
孤单、稚嫩地叫着。
我也坐在冰冷的石凳上，
孤单、稚嫩地望着湖水。

如果我们知道自己就是两只绵羊，
正走在去屠宰的路上，
我会哭泣，你也会哭泣
在这浮世上。

Winter's Day

A wild duck cries on a lake one winter's day
alone and meek
I sit on a cold stone bench
looking at the water, alone and meek

Had we known we were two lambs
on our way to slaughter
I'd weep, you'd also weep
in this floating world

在桥上

一对恋人像两首老歌，
相依在古桥头上。
“ 我喜爱柳树谦逊，
雍容华贵的枝条……
远方苦行僧一样的江水，
没有语言能与它相称。
我想，是我心中长年的哀叹
毁了江水在这里浩瀚，
像逆子把慈母抛弃。
一阵冷风，一阵乌云
是我反反复复的病痛。
我们的爱永久，悲哀亦永久……”
像两首老歌，
心底的苦水使他们紧抱，
像要把各自吞下。

On the Bridge

Like two old songs the lovers
lean on an ancient bridge
I love the humble willow tree
its graceful and lavish branches . . .
The river is a holy man from afar
beyond description
In my heart, years of woes
have ruined this vast river
like a bad son who abandons his mother
Cold wind, black clouds
my perpetual pain
Our love lasts forever, as does our grief . . .
Like two old love songs
they embrace to their chagrin
They swallow each other whole

在清晨

在清晨，一个人挥响了树枝，
“ 起得这么早，去放猪啊？”
我向这辛劳的人问候，他嘿嘿笑着：“去杀猪。”
放猪人甩动树枝：“走，走。”
我的灵魂，街灯，抖动着
像抓着一张自己的逮捕证。
县城静悄悄的，更像那个人手上甩响的树枝。

Early in the Morning

One morning, a man swings a switch
Up so early to herd the pigs?
I greet the hardworking man who giggles, *To kill pigs*
He waves the switch, *Go, go*
My soul, the streetlight, shivers
as if it was clenching its own arrest warrant
Quiet county, more like the switch hissing in his hand

在浮世

野鸭子在半空
沙哑，单调地叫着
“啊！啊！”
多么像我们，
面部安详地走着和坐着，
心里总有一种
朦胧的凶兆，
隐约的担忧……

In the Floating World

A wild duck in midair
cries dryly
Ah! Ah!
So much like us
walking, sitting with calm faces
yet our hearts always
bear a vague threat
a slight worry

夫妇老苦经

她老了，
乳房也耷拉下来，
像一口袋面粉。
他们家乡的河水奔流，
两岸的人民
换了一茬又一茬，
像夏天的萤火虫，
一闪一灭的。
而河水映照月亮的能力
不会有什么变化。
如果我再为无常而悲痛，
我就是一个十分愚昧的人。

A Couple's Old Sutra

She is old
breasts sagging
like bags of flour
River runs through their hometown
People on both shores
change batch after batch
like summer fireflies
that glow and dim
But the river won't change its means
to reflect the moon
If impermanence still saddens me
I must be a fool

古别离

什么都在来临啊，什么都在离去，
人做善事都要脸红的世纪，
我踏着尘土，这年老的妻子
延续着一座塔，一副健康的喉咙。

什么都在来临啊，什么都在离去，
我们因为求索而发红的眼睛，
必须爱上消亡，学会月亮照耀
心灵的清风改变山河的气息。

什么都在来临啊，什么都在离去，
一个人情欲消尽的时候
该是多么蔚蓝的苍穹！
在透明中起伏，在静观中理解了力量。

什么都在来临啊，什么都在离去，
从清风中，我观看着你们，
我累了，群山也不能让我感动，
而念出落日的人，他是否就是落日？

Ancient Departure

They come, they go
A century where man is ashamed of good deeds
I step upon dust, this old wife
still guards a pagoda, a healthy voice

They come, they go
Our eyes grow sore from searching
Embrace death, learn to glow from the moon
Wind from a heart shifts mountains and rivers

They come, they go
When lust is all spent
how blue the sky becomes
Rise and fall in transparency, grasp strength in mindfulness

They come, they go
I watch you in cool wind
I'm tired, even mountains can't inspire me
Sunset speaker, is he the sunset?

述怀

当再没有主题可以宣讲，
人们在这里生活，
却没有办法来安放
各种树，各种花，
各种草，和各种鸟。
人们有这么多珍贵的财宝，
却没有容纳它们的瓶子。
这里的每一件事物
都是他的心灵折射出来的。
各种树，各种花，
各种草，和各种鸟，
如果有一样不是他的心灵，
他就孤立了，
就要在梦幻里，
沉沦到很久……

当再没有主题可以宣讲，
人们在这里生活，
心中都有一种失去了
中心码头的凄凉。
而湖水安静，
仿佛刚遭受完暴力，
折射着他的思想，
没有一丝波澜。
从今往后，
迅捷的水鸟，
混合在苍穹的光里，
变成遥远的钟声，
渐渐冷清，
像你，坐在我身边，
像我，坐在你身边……

Speak, Heart

No more subject to preach
people settle here
with no idea how to settle
trees, flowers
grass, birds
Men possess so many treasures
yet without a vessel to keep them in
Everything here
refracts from a man's heart
Each tree, each flower
each grass, each bird
Should any of these leave his heart
he'd feel isolated
sinking into illusions
for a long time

No more subject to preach
people settle here
with a dreary heart
that has lost its main harbor
The lake is still
as if after some violence
refracting a man's thoughts
without a ripple
From now on
swift water birds
blend with sky light
into distant chimes
colder and bleaker
like you sitting by me
and me sitting by you

悲伤

没有一部作品可以把我变为恒河，
可以把这老朽的死亡平息，
可以消除一个朝代的阴湿。
我想起柏拉图与塞涅卡的演讲。
孔子的游说，与老子的无言。
我想起入暮的讲经堂，纯净的寺院
一柄剑的沉默犹如聆听圣歌的沉默。
死亡，爱情和光阴，都成了
一个个的问题，但不是最后的一个问题。
我想起曙光的无言，落日的圆满。
没有一部作品可以让我忘掉黑夜，
忘掉我的愚蠢，我的喧闹的生命。

Sorrow

No masterpiece can transform me into the Ganges
nor pacify this worn-out death
nor dispel the moldiness of a dynasty
I recall speeches by Plato and Seneca
Confucius's teachings and Lao Zi's silence
I recall dusky scripture halls and chaste temples
A sword's silence, like silence listening to a psalm
Death, love, and time become
questions far from the ultimate
I recall the silence of dawn, the plenitude of a setting sun
No masterpiece can make me forget the dark night
forget my folly, my riotous life

惭愧

像每一座城市愧对乡村，
我零乱的生活，愧对温润的园林，
我恶梦的睡眠，愧对天上的月亮，
我太多的欲望，愧对清彻见底的小溪，
我对一个女人狭窄的爱，愧对今晚
疏朗的夜空，
我的轮回，我的地狱，我反反复复的过错，
愧对清净愿力的地藏菩萨，
愧对父母，愧对国土
也愧对那些各行各业的光彩的人民。

Remorse

Like each city remorseful of the country
my messy life is remorseful of tender gardens
my nightmarish sleep remorseful of the moon
my extravagant desires remorseful of clear creeks
my petty love for a woman remorseful
of a bright sky tonight
my reincarnation, my hell, my repeated wrongs
remorseful of the pure and powerful Ksitigarbha
of my parents, my nation
and those illustrious folks from all walks of life

Notes

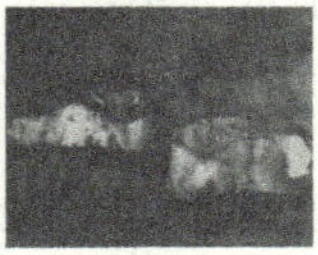

I

"A View from Mount Ho Bridge"
Mount Ho Bridge [Heshan Bridge] is located in Suzhou, Jiangsu Province.

"Tribute to Master Yi"
The title can also be translated as "Respect a Master."

"1967"
Erhu, the traditional Chinese violin, is literally translated as a "two-stringed barbarian instrument." It contains a vertical post attached to a boa-skinned wooden base resonator. The musician plays by pulling a horsehair bow with his/her right hand, horizontally between two vertical strings.

"Toon Tree"
Bengbu is a city in northern Anhui.

II

"Native Soil"
The "tiny beast" is an animal statue placed near the river by villagers since ancient times, as a talisman against evil and floods.

"Mysterious Gratitude"
In Chinese feng shui, a red koi symbolizes longevity, luck, and wealth.

"Locked River Tower"
Locked River Tower [Suojiang Tower] was built in 1558 during the Ming dynasty. It is located in Jiujiang City, Jiangxi Province.

"Motherland"
Guxi River is a downstream tributary of the Yangzi River.

"Great Leap Bridge"
This bridge is located in Ma'anshan, Anhui Province. It was named during the years of the "Great Leap Forward" (1958-1960), a catastrophic campaign launched by Mao Zedong in his attempt to modernize the economy—and "catch up with the West"—through rapid industrialization and collectivization. By the end of the "Great Leap Forward," the estimated death toll was between eighteen and fifty-five million.

For thirteen years, Yang Jian passed by the Great Leap Bridge on his way to work at an air compressor factory.

"Mount Zhen Monastery"
One of the famous ten ancient monasteries in China, Mount Zhen Monastery was built during the Tang dynasty (618-907). It is located in Dangtu County, Ma'anshan, Anhui Province. Much of it was destroyed during the Second Sino-Japanese War (1937-1945). Further devastation occurred during the Cultural Revolution (1966-1976).

A *kasaya* is a robe worn by a Buddhist monk or nun.

"Surveying from Mount Dongliang"
Mount Dongliang is located near the eastern shore of the Yangzi, southwest of Dangtu County in Ma'anshan, Anhui Province.

"Kaishan Bridge"
Kaishan Bridge is located in Suining, Sichuan Province. Yang Jian likes its name which, literally translated, means "open" and "kindness."

III

"Remorse"
Ksitigarbha is a bodhisattva widely revered in China and Japan. Often depicted as a monk with a shaved head, he holds a wish-granting jewel in one hand and a staff in the other. He uses the wish-granting jewel to light the way, and strikes open the gates of Hell with his staff. [See Williams, Paul. "Faith and devotion: the cults of Buddhas and Bodhisattvas." *Mahāyāna Buddhism: The Doctrinal Foundations.* London and New York: Routledge, 1989. 243.]

Yang Jian, *God of Poetry*, 2014. Ink on paper, 43 x 29 cm.

Biographies

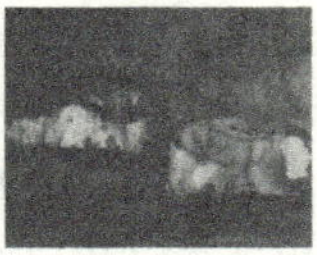

Lauded as one of the greatest Chinese living poets, **Yang Jian** (杨键) writes in the tradition of pastoral poetry. Born in Anhui Province in 1967, he worked as a factory laborer for several years before starting to write in the mid-eighties. He is the author of five volumes of verse: *Selected Poems* (2015), *Weeping Temple* (2014), *Remorse* (2009), *Ancient Bridge* (2007), and *Late Dusk* (2003), the latter rated as one of the nation's top ten titles of the year. His honors include the Liu Li'an Poetry Award, the Rougang Poetry Prize, the Yulong Poetry Prize, and the prestigious Chinese Media Literature Award. Also a prolific ink and wash painter, Yang leads a Buddhist life in Ma'anshan, Anhui.

Fiona Sze-Lorrain is the author of three books of poetry, most recently *The Ruined Elegance* (Princeton, 2016), a finalist for the Los Angeles Times Book Prize, and one of *Library Journal*'s "Best Books 2015: Poetry." She is also a zheng harpist and a widely published translator of contemporary Chinese, French, and American poets. Her work was shortlisted for the 2016 Best Translated Book Award and longlisted for the 2014 PEN Award for Poetry in Translation. She has been named a 2019-2020 Abigail R. Cohen Fellow at the Columbia Institute for Ideas and Imagination. She lives in Paris.

Christopher Merrill has published six poetry collections, including *Watch Fire* (1995), for which he received the Lavan Younger Poets Award from the Academy of American Poets; many edited volumes and translations; and six books of nonfiction, among them, *Only the Nails Remain: Scenes from the Balkan Wars* (2001), *Things of the Hidden God: Journey to the Holy Mountain* (2005), *The Tree of the Doves: Ceremony, Expedition, War* (2011), and *Self-Portrait with Dogwood* (2017). His writings have been translated into nearly forty languages; his journalism appears widely; his honors include a Chevalier from the French government in the Order of Arts and Letters. As director of the International Writing Program at the University of Iowa, Merrill has conducted cultural diplomacy missions to more than fifty countries. He serves on the U.S. National Commission for UNESCO, and in April 2012 President Obama appointed him to the National Council on the Humanities.